MECHANICS·
MERCANTILE
LIBRARY.

Foiled Again

Foiled Again

POEMS

J. Allyn Rosser

WINNER OF THE NEW CRITERION POETRY PRIZE

Ivan R. Dee

CHICAGO 2007

*Funding for this year's New Criterion Poetry Prize
has been provided by the Drue Heinz Trust.*

www.ivanrdee.com

Library of Congress Cataloging-in-Publication Data:
Rosser, J. Allyn (Jill Allyn), 1957–
    Foiled again : poems / J. Allyn Rosser.
        p. cm. — (New criterion poetry prize)
    ISBN-13: 978-1-56663-763-3 (alk. paper)
    ISBN-10: 1-56663-763-5 (alk. paper)
    I. Title.
PS3568.O8466F65 2007
811'.54—dc22
        2007032314

Acknowledgments

Poems included here have appeared in the following
publications: *The Alaska Quarterly Review*: "First Empathy";
The Atlantic Monthly: "Municipal Playground," "Bus to San
Miniato al Monte"; *Black Ridge Review*: "Aftermath," "Spring in
Philadelphia"; *failbetter*: "Discounting Lynn"; *The Georgia
Review*: "Asceticism for Dummies," "Eastern Box," "Early in
Any Century," "Revisiting the City of Her Birth," "Q & A Step
Out"; *The Hudson Review*: "Before You Go"; *Hunger
Mountain*: "Perfect Pitch," "Row of Columns in Rome,"
"*Unterredung mit Franz Lumitzsche*"; *The Journal*: "Marathon";
The Kenyon Review: "Equilibrium Update"; *Literary
Imagination*: "Her Reading of His Letter," "Royal Pain";
Michigan Quarterly Review: "Ode on a Mockingbird"; *Ninth
Letter*: "Lunch Break," "Never Once With"; *Nightsun*: "Letter
to a Young Squirrel"; *Ploughshares*: "China Map"; *Poetry*:
"Death Dance," "Handle," "Internal Revenue," "Literature,"
"Lullaby for the End of the Millennium," "Sea Urchin," "The
Smell of Rat Rubs Off," "Street Boy," "Subway Seethe," "Then
too there is this"; *Slate*: "Strange State, Wrong Highway, Cold
Night," "Unthought," "Fourteen Final Lines"; *The Southern
Review*: "Be the Dog"; *Third Coast*: "Right Moment, Wrong
Soirée"; *TriQuarterly*: "Mother Lets Off a Little Steam."

A number of these poems have been reprinted in the following anthologies or websites: *Best American Poetry 2006*: "Discounting Lynn"; *Never Before: Poems About First Experiences*: "First Empathy"; *Poetry Daily*: "Then too there is this," "The Smell of Rat Rubs Off," "Subway Seethe" (reprinted online); *Poetry Daily Essentials*: "Subway Seethe"; *Verse Daily*: "Equilibrium Update" (reprinted online).

The author would like to express gratitude to the National Endowment for the Arts and the Ohio Arts Council, as well as to the editors of the magazines in which these poems first appeared, sometimes in slightly different form.

Thanks also to Daniel Hoffman and Stephen Dunn for their help and encouragement.

Contents

III

IV

It will flame out, like shining from shook foil. . . .
—Hopkins

I

Fourteen Final Lines

The favored sight is that which disappears.
Wise angels only hum, and hide their wings.
Some toxins will not drain except by tears.
The monkey throws his feces as he swings.
In heroes, it's the flaw that most endears.
We watch the puppet show to spot the strings.
Success occurs when you forget to fail.
Some people seem more naked when they're dressed.
(The garter and bouquet but not the veil.)
He dreams about the smiles she suppressed.
The prisoner doesn't care who makes his bail.
Some stones bleed if resolutely pressed.
The bay leaf is never served with the stew.
I'd never have said this if not to you.

Eastern Box

Like any other revelation, it came
at an inconvenient time: pouring rain,
running late, end of a hectic week.
I pulled over because the last time
I'd vowed the next time I would.
They blunder across the macadam—
you swerve, and later return to find
a shiny wet mosaic of turtle.
This one was smack in the middle,
nudging itself over the double yellow
at an idiotic pace, fool's head out and up.
I bent down and grasped it.
The heft stopped me when I rose.
Now two fools with one head
huddled in the road while my wipers
thunked a thick tattoo, like heartbeats
on carapace, driver's door ajar.
The heft signified more than turtle.
Then I heard and felt it groan:
the intricately hinged doors of the plastron
grinding shut. The shell was smooth
and dark and hard, with blazing
yellow bird's-head glyphs
in perfect symmetry skirting the dome.
It was a high, gleaming dome,

arched in mad exaggeration
of any conceivable terrapin need
for height, drama, dignity.
I kept standing there until
my whole body formed a question,
my future emptied for what might
now fill and direct it, my sometime
soul, my mind, open wide, prepared.
But it had shut. It was staying shut.
As if an ancient, lidded bowl
bearing the jewel-heavy wisdom of the ages
had been proffered, turned over to me.
To me. Right here in rural Ohio.
Then sealed before I could see.
Had I reached for it too casually,
or distractedly? Too dutifully?
How many times has the world
called to me when I was not ready,
how many times have I heard it
groan in just that way, withdrawing,
waiting for me to walk it back to safety
in the culvert grass? To slide into my car,
sodden, disappointed, and slam my own door
as the only viable reply?

Lunch Break

Once the whole world is over,
once God takes it into her head
to get out of the business for good,
just go *yee-ha whoo-eee* completely to town
with the grapes of wrath, stomp it all to pulp,
there will be this swollen, voluptuous silence,
like the endorphinous bath of still air
when the tireless man outside your window
lays down his jackhammer and heads for lunch.
That's what time has seemed like to her:
a constant, consciousness-battering drill
with a high whine behind it, and all our
petty dissatisfactions the crusty rubble
it leaves, and the dream of harmony
a blueprint not just lost in the filthy overalls
but soon blurred to illegibility in the wash
when he forgets to check the pockets.

There will be this luscious, velvety silence.

And for about twenty-five minutes
God will be so glad, so exceeding glad,
until she realizes she doesn't know
how long twenty-five minutes has been.

Bus to San Miniato al Monte

I stood there swaying with nuns,
the only non-nun among them,
swaying with equivalent hips
at the same dips and swerves
in the road we all followed,
thinking in words we all knew.
I felt new, somehow. I felt—*nun*.
I fancied my clean hands
haloing the dirty pole
made it a little bit cleaner.
Oh, we were distinctly aware
which of us was and wasn't one.
They nodded to me nonetheless
as lilies to a too-tall, wayward weed
sharing the same earth and taking
the same breeze-scented sun.
I felt accepted then. Ensistered.
When we arrived at the old church,
how gently we flocked out and in
and all as one looked up to praise
the way it was designed to hold the light.
We halted by the image of the man in pain.
Who would not be fascinated, dismayed?
They knelt and prayed, a sound like sluicing water.
I stayed standing, tall and fallen, as I had been
all along. They left me at the altar.

China Map

I was worn out, lost, and sixteen
in China at 6 p.m., everyone
suddenly in a purchasing frenzy,
when he stopped me with a smile
that just turned me upside down:
gold caps on one side, gaps on the other.
I could tell he was more human
than most people, or more kind.
He was old the way everyone is old
when you're sixteen: maybe fifty, or seventy.
I had passed through the village of pork,
the village of shoes, the village of cotton shirts
and linen. Each few blocks the commodity
changed, the sounds and smells trans-laundered
the air you walked in. He held out to me
a section of the oddly shaped fruit
with a rough, nubbly green rind,
smooth amber glistening inside,
a taste divine, beyond my tongue.
He was a busy man with buyers,
we were smack at the core of the village
of fruit. All of his globes were selling.
I was a ready target, fanning out
the colored bills, raising my brows.
He looked at my hotel's card,

looked into both of my eyes, as if to say
it was going to get dark fast,
and sat us down on two crates side by side,
and stopped his hawking then to draw,
in deft, meticulous detail, a map
to get me back: the splashing fountain
with the fish inside the osprey's mouth,
the statue of the sword-bearing giant,
the dog-legging street that led
to a cat's-paw alley just before the really
sharp turn. When he drew an intersection,
the stoplight had all three circles
with diagonal hyphens radiating out—
and that fountain! He spent a lot of time
making it sparkle on the paper bag
under his knife-sharpened, spit-greased pencil.
I remember his ropy hand veins working.
I remember this fruit I carried back
to my hotel and up the stairs, glowing and round
like the truth. Like the globe of the truth
of everything in the whole wide world.
I didn't know how to go about eating it
when I got back to my room:
no knife, no dish, no napkin.
I sat and watched it ripen in the dusk,
breathing its aroma, which seemed
the antidote to every wrong thing.
In the morning I can't believe I just
left it behind. That fruit.
Also, doubtless, the map.

Strange State, Wrong Highway, Cold Night

Centuries of suffering have led to this,
a warm seat near the fire,
chilled hands curled snugly around
a mug of something hot and good,
no imminent threats, no one squinting
over club or mace or dagger.
The mug is hot enough almost to hurt
the flesh, so one has constantly
but subtly to shift the grip,
letting some surfaces escape
while others brave the heat, so now
the whole body attends, thrills
to the sensation of its two palms,
like sinking into a Japanese bath,
heat seeping through each limb and
agreeably down the spine, along
the phantom tail, all trails meeting
at the center of one's being.
Centuries of deprivation have led
to this merging of animus and animal
who take their ease together
in a burst of health and good will,
so even the voice of Neil Diamond,
insufferable Neil, is suddenly beloved,
or at least forgiven; he gets piped

right into the bath along with
several quaintly dusty artificial roses.
The faint, sharp odor of a cleanser too
is taken in, all of it welcomed
into the bath, the inner streaming.
God knows what horrors my forebears
had to endure so I could choke the engine
and come crunching in imported boots
into Kathy's Country Inn, to settle
near a stranger's fire, to drink a brew
tropical and strong, prepared in exchange
for this green wisp I pull from my pocket,
the convenient bimillennial culmination
of beads and pelts and sacks of grain or gold.
Nothing wanted, no moment lamented:
just being here, as near nirvana as it gets.
One would almost have given up all
for this moment if it hadn't come unbidden.
But it has, and it will retire soon,
perhaps never to return with such
completeness, or if so then rarely.
But why? Why *not* this blessed feeling
every damn day? After all, the drink
needed only be good. And hot.
And one had been merely chilled,
and a little tired, and lost.

Street Boy

The afternoon slows down, the town in steady rain.
That one with the trendy chicken-plucked look—
hair a tufted circle on top, the rest shaved all around—
I can't really care about. Of course I hope
he grows up without totalling himself and his car,
but he's the clown in this act. He seems even
to know his place as unworthy twerpy follower
of the one no one would look away from for long,
whose James Dean stance, hands deep in pockets
of a rattily natty maroon corduroy blazer,
shoves his shoulders nearly to his ears.
Beneath the blazer, long sulked-in jeans,
oversized black boots. He lifts one
to kick a milkshake someone couldn't finish
standing on the sidewalk, and it lands on
its side, explodes and rolls a vanilla graffito,
expletive unfurling. Expressionless himself.
The other boy smirks before the rain douses
and sweeps it stupidly into the gutter.

Even if I were not invisible through this darkish window,
they would know how to erase me. Well, *he* would.
I would enjoy that, just to see how he would do it,
what sort of panache he'd pack in his shrug.

Raining harder, and the tuft-headed one shifts
unhappily under the Revco awning, pivoting
his whole body now and then to see what the one
I'm half in love with's doing, fifteen, maybe sixteen:
he's twitching in sublime irritation, lighting up
again, hard to do with both hands in your pockets
but he pretty much manages no problem, and now
comes the move that gets me. He strides out
from under the awning, a spotted Lucky sticking straight
from his lip, walks two buildings down and turns
at the corner so his back's to Main Street and me,
stands, his twitch becalmed at last, stands
without heeding his friend's pleading
jeering calls, *you idiot, you idiot, you*
idiot, stands hunched, not looking up or down,
and I can tell this is his moment, this is where
he'll break off, he's going to unload everyone,
he doesn't blink as he hawks up their nothingness
and spits, feeling himself filling with what's left:
he takes possession of his spirited bad luck for good
and mounts and rides it without moving a muscle, stands
letting the rain collect behind his collar and drench
his gloriously inappropriately maroon corduroy
and his hair that looks not combable by anyone
alive, wild and bunched even when the rain
has patted keeps patting at it harder and harder
like an obsolete humiliated hand that wants to
feed and fend for and in general do for him,
and he has turned his back at last on the clown,
and on Main Street full of clowns you can both see
and not see, who wouldn't dare try to keep an eye on him
or try to follow him from now on.

Internal Revenue

I have distracted rodents from their cheese,
Lured seasoned sirens with my melodies,
And brought some handsome statues to their knees.
  I could not beguile you.

Having faced your shoulder, back and heel,
Borne the treadmarks of your fortune's wheel,
Felt your indifference to what I feel,
  My heart would not revile you.

I've shelved all my abiding passion, stashed
My childish cares and organized my past:
Real property, junk bonds, trusts amassed.
  —I don't know where to file you.

Royal Pain

It's true, I've thought of you many times.
That's gratifying to hear, isn't it?
Many, many times. Not always fondly.
Oh I know you were not a perfect prick,
or not exclusively such, yet you gave
such a dead-on faithful imitation.
Even then, when I was permitting you to,
I was stunned, impressed. Enough to stay.
Naturally I'd heard stories about pricks,
the sort of thing they're capable of,
but never had experienced one first-hand.
So to speak. It was an education!
I have reviewed those lessons so often,
replaying those scenes night after night,
I feel like some woman who was cast
alongside Olivier, a woman whose name
gets mixed up with Vivien Leigh's.
I was no match for you,
I'm not embarrassed to admit it. At every turn
you upstaged me. Even in memory!
Of course my memory has monkeyed
liberally with the script. By now,
you're so much cleverer, more interesting,
better-looking too, you wouldn't know yourself.
You were so easy to add to, so much missing.

Plus I had to soften some of your gestures
just to make them credible,
and tweak your quips to sustain
my own fascination. By now
you are so much my creature,
I half-expect to receive royalties
each time I hear your name.

Right Moment, Wrong Soirée

I think I may like you, though what you've told me
in this first conversation isn't particularly appealing.
Beneath that mealy-mouthed demeanor
one detects a scent of pith—I'd like to do something
about the yellowy oblong shape of what you
almost said, its freckled, bulbous bottom half,
its too-narrow forehead,
not to mention the silly dish you came in with.
I'd like my attention to slice into you
as into ripe pear,
the season-thinned skin so unresisting,
juiceful flesh dividing like air
from air, not even a formality's worth
of protest, an offering so natural
as not to seem an offer at all:
a given, unagented.
I want invention in one eye and confession
in the other, their cooperation inter-transcendent.
I need your lips to get themselves around
the thing only you could say.
Yes, I'm sure now
I'd like to know that part of you
you've been saving for someone
I'm not, though for all you know
I might be, asking to see you
so wholly and swiftly (let me)
you won't feel a thing.

Never Once With

You were there, whatever that means,
there beside me in the first room,
our atmosphere smoky but sight-
pregnable, so when I looked at you
I saw something other than alarm,
or cause for it, in your position,
the unprecedented tilt of your chin.
Who knew but that you always behaved
as if someone had a hand on your collar?
Both of us gamely drawing straws,
squandering our cache of magic coin, k-
chunk, k-chink, into the ancient well
of the second day we met, which is
what I want to talk about, since the first
can't be recorded in reliable language,
whatever that, you know, means.
The arterial thudding was too loud for us
both to hear clearly, the molecules
wouldn't hold still long enough
to let us be anything but beside ourselves,
beside one another, parallel, not with.
But in that second room,
a rectangle of light aiming down
and away from your shoes, there was
a grim, greasy-banged boy mopping

the facts he wasn't about to let us have,
nope, nope, nope, mopping up,
spreading some awful odor
at our feet from his bucket
to distract us, sloshing stench
in puddles toward our table
as if we deserved that, we were
thinking we were happy, whatever
that means. The sloshing
made a kind of hush,—or hiss,
a cosmic snort of derision.
Like all augurs of ill, the dark-banged boy
did not even look up when we exited,
and in the parking lot where real things
tend to happen more often than elsewhere,
you asked me for a bobbie pin to refasten
the dragging end of one of your plates.
They were illegibly dirty, the car itself
in bad shape, and I had to wonder what decade
you'd hoped for me to come from—
bobbie pins?—and that should have warned me
to adjust the walls, my eyebrows, the lot,
like a tilted frame enclosing an unsigned painting
of a landscape you can only dream of,
but someone's truck's brakes let out
a pneumatic sigh and I got with you
into the car and you were gone taking me
with you, driving and driving, there was no
way to renege, no rest area for untold miles,
the first message already forming
in condensation on the rearview,
the last one in pen on a paper hanger,
swinging in the closet of the third room,
the one we were headed for.

II

Asceticism for Dummies

When it nests in your core, catches
Your inner eye, gooses your heart,
Gleams like a redeeming thing,
Don't love it.

When it feels like heaven in your hands,
Bathes your mind with the scent
Of a still undiscovered wildflower,
Forget it.

When it kisses you, turn away.
When it asks for you, don't answer.
When it croons, moans, whimpers,
Don't admit it.

Should it curve along your hips
The way your hips have always hoped,
Should it fit nicely into your rib cage,
Cut it out.

If it has borne you, dismount.
If it accommodates, move out.
If it comes to bless you (no-brainer) —
Damn it.

But when it blazes up in a field
You're speeding by too fast to see clearly,
To stop at or ever find again, go ahead:
Want that.

Unthought

Every time I'm reminded of the actor
who willed his own skull to repertory
for use as that of poor Yorick
in stagings of *Hamlet*, I wince to think
I forgot his name. Was it Cooke?
Cronin? Cracken?
              Cooke I decide, and
doubt sets in. So the thought I always
nearly have about this morbid legacy
never fully shapes itself. I've almost
had this thought at least a hundred times.
For some reason until I get that name right
I can't permit myself to think it through.
Maddening, like a sneeze that won't quite,
all day it just, climax unbrought-to...
Sir Arthur Cronin seems plausible
until I suspect I've conflated the actor
with Conan Doyle, who solved hard cases
of lives dissolved. Absurd, really,
this paralyzing sense of obligation to a name.
Alas poor whoozis, who'd have given rise
to *some* thought in my still humming skull,
my wracked skull rich with the image of his,
held aloft nightly to shadow forth past performances,
like the echo of a hermit-crab-deserted shell.

Is it still in use? No prop man could throw it away.
Did he love puns? Was he the boneheaded sort
who felt Ophelia must be played by a man
because she would have been in Shakespeare's day?
Did he upstage a friend? Was he gifted enough to?
Sir Something. Arthur, George? Frederick.
It's killing me, since his whole idea was to be
remembered—literally—letting his too solid skull
stand for his love of the curtain-hush, the lights,
the flourish of lines and crushed velvet and the gasp
just audible in the front row; to be a part of it,
a body part of it. The thought I want to have
undoes itself again. You go ahead and think it for me.
I guess I never wanted it. I think that may be why
I had to tell you. Here, take this from me.
You'll think of something. Please. This is as far as I go.

Perfect Pitch

When Dean Martin sings, "Send Me
the Pillow that You Dream on," he is so far
from sounding sincere that it doesn't even
occur to you he might once have meant it,
not even the first time perusing the lyric sheet
over coffee and cannoli, nor while trying it out
in the presence of his latest squeeze
who did way more for him than dream,
and this releases us from all that hooey
about being "true." It's a reason to love him.
And do we? *Encore!* We adore insincerity
as long as it's piled on thick enough
not to question our cultivated jadedness
while sipping at the martini of its hyperbole.
Our real feelings don't come into it.
The songwriter's feelings never came into it.
Purely lovable are Dean's silly vocal fillips,
the light melodic curlicue he adds
like a twirl of clean-shaven mustache,
the heart-shaped moue,
the smiley-face-dotted *i* of his absolute distance
from the song's semantics, while he drips with them,
fingers them back into his shiny black hair.
We love to see him simulate a tipsy weave,
slipping on the fifties-width oil slick of suavity

his tinsel-thin heartstrings are soaking in
while he fondles the mike with a deft twist,
a swizzling motion for all the prop drinks
biographers insist were really apple juice—
not even a genuine drunk!—
his gesture flanked by flashy cufflinks
like gold quotation marks around his act:
every eye-roll, wink, triply rehearsed
doubletake and limp-kneed moan
when the pretty legs walk lavishly away.
Nothing in that creamy maraschino manner
pretends to so much as an inch of depth.
How refreshing in a land rich with charlatans
to find one so pure, so true to his métier
he sells nothing but his perfect sales pitch,
seduces us for nothing but a counter-quirk
of eyebrow, and the rapt half-smile
that can't quite summon the indifference
of a smirk.

Marathon

When did the day begin, when the people assembled?
When the sun bared its breast? When the tripod
was unfolded, when the lens was uncapped?
And when did she arrive, this raggy girl
sitting on the sidewalk as if she'd been here
always, bearing the news in bold letters
that humanity is on its last legs? We *know*.
How long, how long have we known?
A man of proud bearing bows to his own leg,
heel propped confidently on a public waste barrel.
I cast away the trash of my days, he thinks,
praying to some arcane muscle deity: Thoccus,
god of hamstrings. Mohor, god of quads.
Other leg. Nike, Adidas, gods of commods.
I have my spritz bottle, my heart, whatever
Janette thinks she can do to it, I have
the sun on my back and I cast myself
headlong into the future without reflection
or pettiness. I shed all longings, all, all
but one: to move smoothly through space
ahead of my fellows.
                         Another man clutches himself
briefly before us all. A woman reaches back
to tug at a shoulder blade. Wingless, moled.
An underling from the local station is repositioning

a tripod for the videocam pulsing with light.
He will record the event as if to say, without overt
envy or judgment, Lo, these persons do now
what we do not. The sun adjusts. A banner
is hoisted across Union Street where it meets Court,
the pigeons shuffling, the scent of Colombian Roast,
the air jammed with deep breaths, the milling.
One has had to be here. *This* town, *this* square.
And now: the loosening of the limbs.
A herd of short-necked giraffes wearing neon shorts,
thinks the cameraman wanly. Three times fast.
Someone's sister's pain in her head
worries her. Always the same spot behind the ear.
When did she first feel it? The pistol will go off
and our Birks-shod, tri-scarved Cassandra
will sneer sweetly and stand up at last.
The pigeons will startle and, as quickly, settle.
A man stands ostentatiously stretching
in that unmistakably pregnant posture, palms flat
on the lower spine. He's happy, ready. His wife
really is with child, she will not run. The pistol
will go off and her husband will wave, loping away
as if to hunt and gather things that either sprint
or ripen very quickly. The pigeons seem driven
to get underfoot, disdaining greasy napkins,
propelled by urgent agendas. What do they seek?
And how did all this begin? What point
shortest distance between be this from what other?
A woman sneezes as if shot by the pistol
when it goes off comparatively faintly,
but still the herd lurches forward, seeming a bit
embarrassed to be obeying this signal together
so crowdedly, all in the same direction.

Giraffes at the edge make easier prey for the young lion,
he thinks who readies his videocam. Remind him:
a modest job and salary puts you in the middle
and no one wants you fired or dead. Unless
you provoke ire in any of many other ways.
One might be to sit on the sidewalk
during a crowded marathon; one might be to run
for the sake of your legs, your surging healthfeel,
your vanity while your wife stands rooted,
needing company. Perhaps she is sad,
not just pregnant. The pigeons seem to recall
better times, and are disdainful of it all:
the pistol shot, the clabber of sneakers,
the very idea that they are disdainful. Deliberately
they scatter, in waddly hops and wing-snorts.
Next year will be better, the banner will say
32nd Annual, they are already lowering it
and she sneers. The banner was only up
for half an hour, tops. Our videoboy will be
spared an early promotion. The sister must still have
aspirin in her bag. The end of the world
will wait for another raggy girl with more vim
and less attitude to announce it. The computers
will be down. Someone will be first and someone
last in the race, there will be a replay of the finish
but not of the start, you'd think it would tell us
something, never ever of the start.

Discounting Lynn

I find it in the twenty-five-cent bin,
which I browse biweekly for the book
that will explain why my hand
seems so misty lately, even
with my new glasses on,
why it can't hold on to anything
with the grip of commitment,
not even a fork which looks
unsettling these days
like half a set of silver teeth
so I bend down low and I choose.

This book has been through a lot.
Since it's poetry, I imagine
it had trouble finding a publisher,
so now rub in this further indignity:
abandoned by the bookseller
at a discount of 25%, and then
dumped by the first owner for profit
in a used bookstore ($9.70—
how pathetic, not even $9.99)
relegated then to an even more desperately
used bookstore ($2—handwritten
on a round orange sticker)
and now given up for lost, now

25¢ slashed sloppily in pencil on the flyleaf.
The book looks fairly readable, a Lynn
wrote it. Maybe not, though, maybe just
a pseudonym. Actual name possibly
Lila-Jean, someone trying to abridge
her native floridity, sound more seriously
friendly, solid, actual, northern.

I find the right spot to read this book:
under an oak tree whose acorns are so small
they seem toy-like underfoot, scattered by a child's
imagination, not capable of reproduction
or supplying half a squirrel's midnight snack,
here beside the Muffler 'n Brake Shop
and two dumpsters. Stacked railroad ties
form a half-bench beneath the tree.
A place where you can smoke a cigarette
and in effect throw yourself away
to prepare for reading this thrice-junked text.
On the backleaf some notes are scribbled
by one of the owners, presumably the first,
who invested the most to read the book
and needed a return on that investment.

many characters are doing something on the page

I don't mind the lack of punctuation, but I do
like a thought and I think
how fortunate I rescued this book
from such a dodo:

book draws you out of the text

and really it says *texl* because she was so
done with this book she couldn't bother
to cross her *t*. Well honey good riddance.
I can't help thinking she. Does some post-
Paleolithic, prefeminist corner of my psyche
suspect that men still tend not to buy
slender poetry paperbacks by Lynns?
But at least there's some substance
to that note and I read some pages to see
if there's anything in it. Could be.
What if this Lynn were to become our era's
Dickinson? What if she already is!
Then I start writing this because my hand
feels misty again, "Lynn" hasn't helped
one jot. Nor has anti-Lynn, or whoever
said the words Lynn's ex-reader wrote,
since it could have been a professor
with a name like a sneeze. Dr. Hatchitt.
I write this on the backleaf, weaving in
and out of his/her scribbles. Then I relent
because an author can't be blamed for her
readers and turn to the last page of texl,
where authors tend to plant their most
magic beans, and just as I'm getting
to the sentence that is about me, I'm
stung on the back of the hand by a sweat bee.
But the sentence turns out to be about Lynn,
Lila-Jean, not me. And I'm not sweating at all,
or I wasn't then, and officially that was no bee.

Letter to a Young Squirrel

It's never about how many nuts,
though I'm not one to say it hurts
to have a trunkful, and a few
stashed underground. Maybe too
some seeds, a thistle. Diversify.
You know the others would sooner die
than praise a single thing you've got.
They'd let it go to rack and rot
before admitting you'd done well.
Let them go to hell.
It can't be a question of resenting
station, since we're all tenanting
the same scrawny, pest-infested
neck of woods, scrimping nests
from nothing, strips of scratch
that stink when wet and must be patched
each year. Each year we're overcome
with all the piling up. Numb
from fatigue, but still the chatter
starts in. Gibes, digs. Nothing sadder.
What eats at them could eat at you.
What can you do?
Avoid the highest perch. And *run*.
Always bolt across the lawn.
Never look over your shoulder.

Get busy, stay busy. Act bolder
than you are, and keep your claws clean.
Don't be too friendly. Don't be mean.
You can't win! This sounds harsh,
but what are we? Tussocks in the marsh
of time. A skittish question mark
in low profile. (Avoid the park.)
Just look at that oak-fed fool
chuffing his beady mug at you,
like a mad setter with a cough.
You're new: he wants to scare you off.
Why can't they all just climb together
in peace? *Why* must one be better?
Why won't Chuck say where he finds
the pink soft filmy stuff that lines
his nest? You didn't see? It glows
in the dark! Bastard just goes
rigid, fixes me now with one,
now the other eye. Both half gone.
You're young: don't think too highly of
your nuts. Don't puff your cheeks with love;
you'll wear them out. Remember this:
Invest in work. All else is risk.
Go on, get cracking. Just watch me.
And stay away from my tree.

Be the Dog

I
The administrative assistant stands serenely
  with her green cloth coat on, Friday, 5:02.
Her boss taps his Mont Blanc, mentioning
  the misdirected invoice for the eighth time.
She knows he has recently been responsible
  for losing a prized client. He will work late tonight.
He will come in early on Saturday, maybe also
  Sunday afternoon. Her eyes narrow slightly:
She will have her work cut out for her, he says
  with ill-disguised pleasure. It is hard to tell
whether her eyes suppress a smile of compassion
  or amused contempt. By the time she leaves
the close elevator for the cool, shining, marble walk
  to the weekend, it's compassion.

II
The big brother scorns the little brother
  in a voice that cracks.
How does he expect to ever make the team
  if he's going to dribble like a girl?
The little brother doesn't really care
  about basketball. He watches.
Will his big brother have to sit on the bench
  again during Saturday's big game?

Afterward, will they clown around at the pizza place?
  Now try it! He dribbles, shoots and misses,
almost glad, almost relieved to hear the curses
  cracking in the air above his head.

III
Two women sit in the park. One is nodding softly,
  inhaling the rich, shimmery air of April.
The statuesque one is successful in the theatre,
  fairly well known. Her clothes drape her precisely
as she counsels her old friend: *...an outrage!*
  Promise me you'll quit, start your own business.
The other one smiles with grateful skepticism
  and toys with the dustjacket of a book
balanced on her lap, as if it were the book
  she is going to write about her friend
in which she will fondly describe the statuesque
  features, the grand, reckless gestures
and the clear voice hardened by too much speaking,
  or too much being listened to.

IV
Twenty feet away, a tired-looking man says MAX!
  as his labrador, growling, bobbing its head
playfully, chomps on the leash in its mouth,
  snarling and wagging, yanking the man roughly on
as if to say, I know what it is to be master
  without which knowledge
I would not have agreed, believe me,
  to be the dog.

Subway Seethe

What could have been the big to-do
that caused him to push me aside
on that platform? Was a woman who knew
there must be some good even inside
an ass like him on board that train?
Charity? Frances? His last chance
in a ratty string of last chances? Jane?
Surely in all of us is some good.
Love thy bloody neighbor, buddy,
lest she shove *back*. Maybe I should.
It's probably just some cruddy
downtown interview leading to
a cheap-tie, careerist, dull
cul-de-sac he's speeding to.
Can he catch up with his soul?
Really, what was the big crisis?
Did he need to know before me
whether the lights searching the crowd's eyes
were those of our train, or maybe
the train of who he might have been,
the person his own-heart-numbing,
me-shoving anxiety about being
prevents him from ever becoming?
And how has his thoughtlessness defiled
who I was before he shoved me?
How might I be smiling now if he'd smiled,
hanging back, as though he might have loved me?

The Smell of Rat Rubs Off

Once again you've fallen for the lure
of his deference, his quick eyes' brightness
slinking from the pantry of the righteous.
Nothing half so sleek as self-licked fur.
Not that he forgot your boots, or left
A single high-aimed compliment unturned.
He'll double back, affect to be concerned
when he's the secret reason you're bereft,
embracing you with his Houdini hold,
repeating chewed-off bits of what you say
so he seems loyal, you the turncoat jay.
You'd think by now you'd learn to be consoled
to know the soul he sold's not yours but his,
though where yours was a hollow feeling is.

Aftermath

Smiled, *smiled* at loathsome Smits
but managed to avoid handshake
of guy who told hooker joke
to Therese, pretty good though,
sorry pal; remembered to thank Peggy
but reminded John of match
he lost, so sure he'd won that;
spilled wine on ivory carpet
but foresight to drink white;
left Therese in boring clutches
of Brad Hitchens, tax breaks;
but good restraint only shrugged
when she claimed I was "weaving,"
wasn't; left without kissing woman
with maroon lips slit skirt thigh
but pressed against on way out;
why the smile, Smits didn't first;
Helen a looker but that house,
jerrybuilt ostentatious & she
still squinty from lift, Therese could tell;
odd, own loathing tripled by own smile;
lost keys but found quickly
this time, ran light but remembered
to fill tank, Sunday night, back roads,
Smits still holding his promotion

over me, as if I cared,
and then to make a crack like that
thank god Therese not there
would never let live down;
still, the twit knows his Nasdaq;
made love maroon lips in mind;
will try to get market tip next time, but
no smile, not from me again he won't.

Her Reading of His Letter

I hope you are well and happy, or happier, and that
you're still at this address. I'm writing this
instead of a list of resolutions — remember
we always did that after midnight? *or happier*
Because we forgot, or put it off, or were at some party
I couldn't wait to get home with you from
because talking with you felt more eventful
than the events we talked about, and heading
for bed at a reasonable wee hour seemed
prematurely mature, you laughing at my repeats
from the previous year, since your lists were
completely new every blessed time, as if not only
had your priorities shifted but the world too,
reassembled into a completely different one
to get home with you from, each time leaving
number one blank. *or happier* One we'd expressly
keep secret. I'm finally dating again.
We have been apart so long now. I'm looking
at the snapshot of you taped above my desk
(the one from that day at the lake, purple sweater)
dating again the only photo in my office,
so you are here with me, *apart so long now*
around and among me, among all the selves
I have auditioned since you left. *the only photo*
Which one would you like the most, I wonder:

43

the well-dressed workaholic who walks his dog
with the resolute heart of a store clerk
the day after Christmas? *the only photo*
Or the vaguely hopeful man-of-leisure in corduroy,
gunning the remote he aims over one knee
from his usual position at the end of the blue sofa
that seems so much longer than before, or
happier gunning and gunning as if
the program he longs for exists a little higher
up the channel bar, higher, accelerating
so what he zaps can't be checked properly,
apart so long now to ensure that when he gets to the end
he can hope he's missed it and start again.
How about this sharp-eyed guy in sweats
rolling his empty cart through the all-night aisles,
alertly scanning shelves because at two a.m.
the overhead glare feels good, it suits his mood,
and he knows *dating again* if he doesn't stay focused
he will overlook *that day at the lake* something essential.
Happy New Year. *or happier* Much love,
so long now

III

First Empathy

The pig on the page is crying.
Its back is angled toward the reader,
but we can still see the squinch
of its features in profile, the three
huge tears gushing diagonally upward.
Its kite is stuck in the tree.
And from somewhere below the crown
of her head, an inch from my lips,
my daughter cries out: "Yeah! Yeah! *Yeah!*"
She is pointing frantically at the pig,
at the kite, using the only one
of her fifteen words that comes close:
"Yeah! Yeah! *Yeah!*" as if to say
I've been there! I know this!
Story of my LIFE!
Her eighteen months' worth of sorrow
wells up in her throat, stuck there
like that kite with its diamond shape
that turns out not to be one,
even diamonds are not shaped like diamonds,
and hearts, it's all going to accrete so slowly,
the midden of quotidian disappointment,
wadding up the string and crumpling
the kite and blocking the passage
of her future joys, for life, hers and

mine to be spent watching. Now
the finger-in-the-dike wail:
she's actually holding back sobs
for this dumb little pig wearing shorts
and I can't stop this. Can't retrieve the kite.
I try to turn the page, but she slaps it back down
with a peremptory dumpling hand.
"Yeah! Yeah! *Yeah!*" One sob.
But there are other pictures of pigs,
I say idiotically, happy pink pigs
eating roast beef and smiling ones
who run their own deli counters
selling low-salt turkey instead of ham,
and pigs with snazzy convertibles,
pigs with jobs on ladders painting,
important pigs running for the bus
bearing briefcases, vacationing pigs
in green jeeps, look! Nothing doing.
She has identified this page as hers.
"Yeah! Yeah!" That kite is stuck in the tree.
"*Yeah!*" We both sit here and stare.
Christ. It is never going to come down.

Municipal Playground

The shockingly green, gold and red beetle—
too petite for a June bug, with greater iridescence
and a delicacy of limb and feeler
unprecedented in the insect kingdom—
walks up her palm to the inside of her wrist.
"I must show this bug to that boy,"
she says of a sulking preadolescent
I've peripherally watched abuse
the for-toddler-only rocking horses
on their rusty springs.
He is the wrong boy.
The beetle, sensing danger, flies off
before I have to make excuses
for the boy's inevitably sour
or mocking or violent response.
Yes, the beetle flies away,
probably wanting his mom to make him lunch,
we decide, heading for the car,
but the boy has noticed her glances,
her interest, watches her with a malevolence
I hope I'm imagining. He waits
and will be there again tomorrow
or next week, and she will approach
with her wistful only-child smile,
her delighting eyes,
to show him something else.

Literature

Yesterday I sat on the sofa with my girl
and struggled with my illustrations of a pig
for a book she wanted to read that no one
had written. Meanwhile there was a poem
I wanted to get on paper that was lost.
It's gone. This is not the poem I mean.
That one would have been much better.
I will never write that poem now,
and I could use a good poem to cheer me up.
Couldn't you? No one else will ever read
Piggy and Dad and the Doctor.
I'm not complaining, I don't think.
I love doing things for my girl while
she still lets me call her my girl.
Blonde ringlets, favors gruyere cheese
and will probably stop saying aminals
when she turns six in a few months.
When little Charley was about to turn six,
Dickens locked himself in a room
with a conjuror's book and paraphernalia,
studying how best to turn a box of bran
into a guinea pig, wring doves from gloves.
Two solid, frustrating days he worked on this—
a few years before he wrote *Dombey and Son*—
two whole days putting aside *Martin Chuzzlewit*,

not a great book, but he didn't know that yet,
so his son's party would be a success;
and, due to Dickens's unparalleled patter,
it was. He kept every child in stitches
though he was, by all accounts, a lousy magician.
This sacrifice may have been what ruined *Martin Chuzzlewit*,
got him on the wrong track, made him impatient
when he returned to it, made him slam America
with too heavy a fist to leave the impression
of good satire. He must have understood the risk.
He must have loved that Charley.
Or the idea of loving him.
More than one of his offspring insisted that he
knew his fictional children better than his own.
When he killed off little Paul Dombey
(years before the death of young Dora
in *David Copperfield*, after whom he would
later name his daughter Dora [who then died
in infancy]) he walked the streets of Paris all night
to mourn him. The rest of his restless life
Dickens could not hear the whisper of waves
on the shore without grieving for Paul.
It took his fictional Mr. Dombey twenty years
(by which time Charley was turning ten)
to understand that his children lived beyond
the fictions he'd made of both of them.
By that time one was dead, and at that point
in the novel I could not wait for my own child
to go to sleep so I could get back to Paul's
surviving sister Florence, whose piteous neglect
needed my attention. She wanted desperately to die
so that her father would finally think
fondly of her, as he did of little dead Paul.

While at the top of the house in my study
I imagined stroking Florence's cheek to sleep
with a hand damp with my actual tears,
my child had a nightmare in which, my husband
told me over eggs the next morning, I had died.
But isn't it my capacity to feel for Florence,
an empathy shaped and nurtured by literature,
that taught me how to love my girl? So then
why do I feel so strange, so removed
from my own life where she sleeps not yet six
down the hall, not quite subconsciously
but faintly quasiposthumously enjoying
the real grief I feel writing this down on paper?
After discussing the dream with her, my husband
went to bed and fell asleep with the light on
while I shivered to see the darkening house
of Dombey and Son fall to ruin, as Dickens
walked the streets of Paris and returned
to the candle burning, his quill dipping again
and again in the inkwell of the same night
I finally joined him, turned off the light and slept too.

Revisiting the City of her Birth

It's true, the Twain Faulkner Dickinson Whitman
team in the cafe's mural has been replaced by
Kafka Neruda Hughes Tagore Hurston
in this Barnes & Noble five and a half years later.
But the same interchangeably overqualified servers
talk ironically of orals and bad C.D.'s over blasts
of cappuccino foam. The parking lot remains
on the western side of the store, the great windows
still face it and the evening sun, the books are still
deliciously too many and free until you buy them.
But the books I've piled before me are not the ones
I panicked over then, like *What to Expect When You're
Expecting*: Epstein's Bar, Peristelic something, lead-painted cribs.
I have a thriving 5-year-old girl, the very one I'd feared,
the one I can't really take my eyes off ever.
She's never been here before. Shamelessly I've bought
an hour for $4.99, a sticker book with fairies
and unicorns, vulgar indulgence after our day
at the museum, and she points out that one fairy
(praying) is clapping for a performance somewhere
beyond the page's perimeter. And I inward do clap too
to have survived the colic thrush projectile vomiting
that never happened, not one not once, and all the semi-
awful things that did, to get to this tranquil moment
when I have the freedom to read. I can read!

I can be who I was, and have my cake too, just read!
She is singing softly to herself, her hair ablaze.
People at nearby tables point her out to their friends,
not like understandably antichildren booklovers
but like enchanted people on a page of unicorns, charmed.
I can read.
                    But just now I don't feel like it.
I'd rather stare at that unconscious cheek with a tint
Renoir would weep to get right, at the fingers
trying to be nimble, try to seize the exact second
her melody segues from "Spoonful of Sugar" into
McCartney's "Two of Us," I who have always hated pink
enjoying her passion for it, feeding her passion
with cotton-candy cloud stickers, and I wonder
why I ever wanted to read a book, such a time-
consuming life-draining impediment, precisely
what I feared she'd be when I allowed myself
to admit I feared her, before she showed her face.

Or was it really this I feared? My own capacity—*desire*—
to dote, this slipping into type, as into a book I never
even dreamed of liking, the rapid snap and suck
of a positive magnet to a negative charge?
I stack tidily between us the books I will not read.

Mother Lets Off a Little Steam

I don't know how I'm expected to get anything done
with these two constantly at odds, cranky sisters
in the backseat on a long ride to the wrong place.
Muse wants the Tunnel of Love on a roller coaster,
and to be spirited there on something more elegant
than a carpet. She'd better marry rich, is all I can say.
Truth wants a deserted rest area with a flat rock to sit on.
I'm not kidding. This is what she'd like the most.
A view of flat rock from a seat of flat rock.
There's a scuffle. "Do I have to stop this car or what?"
But I'm going seventy, we're late, it's rush hour.
Muse pops up in the rearview, rhinestone ruby shades
bouncing painful darts of light into the corner of my eye.
"I have to go again," she hiccups. It's a ruse.
She wants, as always, a new gewgaw, a rainbow slurpee,
or one of those impossible-to-lick-seriously huge lollipops.
Her candy breath reaches and nearly sickens me.
Whereas Truth is so stolid, so smugly abstemious,
it makes you want to shake her hard, knock that wiser-than-
you-know gaze askew, disturb the pristine implacability
of those conspicuously ringless hands folded in her lap.
Placid as a cow in the shade on a hot day.
Oh I love them, you know, but on days like this —
"Sit down," Truth says, levelly. "Try and make me!"
In terms of strength you wouldn't want to put your money

on Muse. Truth has always been a good eater,
fond of climbing outdoors. Built like a moose.
Her sister craves exotic sauces and chocolate,
and some weird combinations of tart and savory,
but try getting her to eat one pea. One grain of plain rice.
She's slight in form but tricky, reckless, unpredictable,
and in certain situations this defeats Truth,
who simply has to be right about everything.
So in spite of her years and her methodical,
relentless scrutiny, she often misses the point.
Meanwhile her sister will just up and blurt something
that at first makes no sense, but then it turns out
to be astonishingly right, the more you think about it.
That's what really ticks off Truth, when we say
"the more you think about it." Her eyes narrow
and her face just sort of shuts down. You pity her then.
She likes her facts neatly stacked on the table.
Muse shrugs a lot, changes sides like a fish,
isn't fazed by paradox. I think she thrives on it.
"Sit," Truth says again, "DOWN." "Why should I,
you're just jealous because I'm taller than you."
"You are *not*." "Am too." "Are not." "My head
almost touches when I stand but you have to stoop,
so I'm taller." "No way." "My eyes are higher. See?"
There is a muffled thump. "Don't make me stop this car,"
I say stupidly, but what else can I do? Muse snickers,
Truth snorts softly. I can't help it, I keep going,
"I'm never taking the two of you with me anywhere
ever again!" "Okay," says Truth. "Fine with *me*,"
Muse sings out. Now they're in league I can't win.
They know perfectly well that without Muse there is no vehicle,
without Truth no road.

Spring in Philadelphia

It is really spring, mid-morning,
I'm feeling happy in the park
under the sky's full blue belly
with my little boy, this boy
who's so jazzed on pancakes,
racing to kneel at each
curved glint of glass he finds
embedded in crumbly soil
the color of old cement
between blades of city grass
too spindly and rough
to be termed leaves. I point
at the only brightness here:
"Look at all the dandelions!"
hoping to distract his fingers
for a while, and he lands on
the cluster I've shown him
but "*Dandelions?*" he says,
stopping short. Do I have any
real authority? "Dandelions."
I stare him down, though
I'm feeling shaky, knowing
full well the language is all wrong,
even the word *boy* seems ludicrous,
what can I do? Even the word *sky*,

the word *son* but by now
he's yanking me yellow to yellow,
yelling "DANDELION!"
and "Look, two! three!"
accruing a visionful for when
we return together to our house —
though it's actually an apartment
we don't own and the city
is fairly unfamiliar to me still,
smelling more like diesel than spring,
and he's not my son, not really,
though he often forgets
and calls me *mommy* and I
sometimes forget and answer.

Equilibrium Update

Look there, a man caught smack in the middle of his life
and almost aware of it; not quite yet resigned
    but past most of the old impatiences, having
developed a consciously casual walk, not quite
  the swagger of yore, nor the dignified limp
to come; rather like a man carrying a long heavy plank,
    glad of his hard-won, admittedly modest momentum;
calmly dreading several varieties of misstep
    such as tipping the future a little too far forward or
letting the past plunk down heedless behind; or merely
    looking down; or turning so quickly to look back as to
whack the one just now bending to pick up her own burden;
  still staunchly bearing it onward in splinterless grip
across the rooftop lifescape—bicep, trapezius and thigh muscles in
play, also those of the spine, the upper lip,
    he is at last in control, yes, in his element, in his heart
    of hearts wondering how long he will bear it, where to and,
as ever, what for.

Then too there is this

joy in the day's being done, however
clumsily, and in the ticked-off lists,
the packages nestling together,
no one home waiting for dinner, for
you, no one impatient for your touch
or kind words to salve what nightly
rises like heartburn, the ghost-lump feeling
that one is really as alone as one had feared.
One isn't, not really. Not really. Joy
to see over the strip mall darkening
right on schedule a neon-proof pink
sunset flaring like the roof of a cat's mouth,
cleanly ribbed, the clouds laddering up
and lit as if by a match struck somewhere
in the throat much deeper down.

Handle

Like the handle of a shovel stuck in a mountain of sand
containing the name of one who had quietly slipped
your mind...
                    haunting unbudgeable shovel jammed
in a mountain of everything unplanned, tipped
up at an angle ungrippable without
falling—someone you meant to get back to,
make sense of, dig gently firmly out
and do right by, as if you could rescue—
the name gaining surge, force, significance
from sheer numberlessnesses of grains
of neglect, the alp of everyone avalanch-
ing back on your little shovelful of names,
halfway up the landfill of those you have failed
in the mountain of slippage you climb,
that every day from now on is a failed
attempt to mount or descend in time.

IV

Sea Urchin

When the mind fumbles, reaching feebly
back and back with its long black needles
waving like one too few or far too many
mutely clacking, poison-tipped antennae
at a wavery something in the past
it cannot now grasp,
lurching vaguely along the ocean floor,
flailing, in a near-despair so pure,
despair of ever again coming across—
no matter how it turn and toss
and turn—that perfect, pink anemone
that lit once up the waste of sea

like muted lightning brightening all

and when distracted by present demands
of now too easily stirred-up sand,
and buffeted by this bad tiding or
that conventional big fish gliding
regally by; when failing at last to find
what it almost once had, the mind,
about to give up on stealth and chance,
has half a heart to pounce
on the first pretty bit of coral
and settle for a self-inflicted epidural,

deadening desire. But never mind.
That's not how it's designed.

Row of Columns in Rome

The columns stand there all day long as if
it were all night, centuries past needing
to shrug off the weight of the actual.

They stand. They stand for what is not now here.
Historians guess at what their makers thought
the years that were to come would not undo.

The columns stand there, stand there all night too,
not interested in the least. How still they hold
the massive heat of day, understood.

Time-locked, time-pocked, they stand straight in a row.
They stand in a row. They stand for one another
and absently take roll. Here. Here.

They seem proud to us, being proud ourselves
to stand tall in the center of something big,
though we are small, always bent on something else.

Back then it seemed the sun beat down hysterically,
beat and beat as if it mattered, on the gone
monument they held for years on end.

The sun still strikes them that way.

Death Dance

oh it is a slow unpartnered one
so anyone could join in any time
the rhythm one you've known
their hands outstretched as if in fond
invitation but only undulating
drawing gravity upward to fingers
sketchy at the far end of their arms
nudging the air aside who needs it
when you can leap this lengthily
without touching down or having to rise
higher than a hope for more hope or
maybe less   maybe less
the music unfamiliar but not
the sway the rhythm the way
you understand sex when you see
jellyfish pulsing along inside the waves
the rhythm one you've known
how to deny the pull of these limbs
in thrall to a new curve in the light
to their own giving in to their own
shadows inking something dark and true
on the walls unreeling behind you
a rhythm the rhythm one rhythm
the ballroom backing away the floor
receding at your first step
one you have known

Q & A Step Out

Q and A didn't stick around after the lecture.
"How about that little bar on the corner
with the pinkish spider plants in the window?"
Q asked, and they went out together,
A just a bit too far ahead of Q on the stairs.
A ordered a gin and tonic with plenty of ice.
He was the kind of guy Q could imagine
doing a hundred situps with no one watching.
Q himself was more or less a Sunday jogger
who stopped to check for tadpoles in the pond.
He asked for a martini, not too dry, with onion.
Q was still thinking about the lecture, and that
got him thinking about all the other lectures.
"Do you think we'll ever get anything straight?"
"That's just what I was despairing about," said A.
They sat silent for a moment while A slumped,
morosely painting a thick tic-tac-toe grid
in the table condensation, x-ing the center.
"Why do I always have to be O?" asked Q.
"You don't have to be O. There need not
be an O. Let's say there is no O."
"Well this is the thing," Q pursued, poking
softly at the onion, "Do you think you have ever
once uttered a single, solitary, irrefutable—?"
"Exactly. Every time I open my mouth

I'm hoping it's for the last time," A said.
They looked at a basketball game on a big screen
above the bar. Either the defenses were great
or the offenses were bad. It stayed *0-0*.
Then came a commercial break
to demonstrate how a woman with bright teeth
would straddle a motorcycle in a swimsuit.
"Now there, what do you think of *her*?"
"I think," A averred, "it's best to try not to."
"Because you'd never, not in a million years — ?"
"Because even if you did you wouldn't. Either
you would be humiliated and not have it,
or you would have it and it would be over."
"And you wouldn't have it again?" "Statistics."
They watched as she sped away, hair like a flame.
"Okay," said Q, "okay okay, but the rest?
Breathing, consciousness, communication,
what's the point in the whole rest of that?"
"The point," A said patiently, as if they'd been through this,
taking a moment to cube-shake-drain the rest of his G&T,
"is to have known all along what the point is."
"You either miss the boat or you're already on it?"
Q asked, though almost afraid to. Then he asked
the waiter for another round without noticing
A had buttoned his coat and was already settling the bill.

Unterredung mit Franz Lumitzsche
[Translate This Page]

Welcome, Mr. Lumitzsche, we are curious
that you bring out always two for where
others draw one. Does it fall you heavily?

It is to be hardly still seen in this hour,
but the main taking up is down come.
I could find examples, if you will like:
sentimental melodies, wrong tales,
thus to enough. Church bells.
In the country of unlimited spaces,
one sti,ens against a touch.
But when the old rains rehearse our soil,
here do we ravel and stretch.

Does the city please you so well?

I am come to Hamburg because of Marya,
with her I would have gone also to Romania.
to Marshall Islands. I accept also Warsaw.
To some one must anscheichen oneself as to a bird.

Is this a happiness which is long to come?

Yes. At first there is creak but no door.
Starting from 40 you have the face

which you earnings/services, and the voice
which you earnings/services.
One needs finally one.

Does this one agree with you at the skins?

Marya, yes. With her I would also have come
to Madagascar, to Greenland. Why?
One is chicken, other fish. We choose.
To question other more is asking fire.

To hear you say such we think on this:
you look to lack the camel of custom.

I do not smoke already an eternity any longer.
To drink was many heavier. What am I
to say to it? These pulling mirrors
and map-cheaters cannot answer.
I am not cinema star, that shows its new dentures
and the new face every five weeks.
No more am I myself when I return.
That is part of my basic disturbance.

There have undertaken whisper that the pails
of what you came for have not filled.
How does that function within you?

I do not take that so importantly.
At times I am zynisch, times inside the vein.
You will hear them paint my brow outside
the circle, yes, be that as true, with Marya
I would also come to the devil, my both feet planted
in fondly hoping it firm ground.

Others have scratched their voices on this
and finally deserved themselves, well beglueckt.
I hope that also succeeds to me.

*Thank you Mr. Lumitzsche, and may we encounter
in future what you will not take only for yourself.*

Thank you.

Ode on a Mockingbird

Lithe shadow, organic jukebox, sly note-taker,
twirling your vocal cords about
like the rainbowy ribbons of a Maypole,
what do you love? *do you love? do you love?*
I've let the birdfeeder level drop down,
but you stay on, enraptured, giddy.

Look: I'm not the type to call a poem song
or waste ink on what a bird might "think."
But *this* one! When he pauses, tips his
fragile, drab tail at the sky, pauses,
then lets fly his *fly his fly his*—hey!
He has reasons. He's selective,
doesn't juxtapose the same way
each time around. He seems to swivel
with the wind from song to song
(though the weathercock's is one
he can't be bothered with); each
a dead ringer for the source.
You can almost hear other birds tisking:
That show-off, faker, no-count,
cheap bastard of a bird, just who
does he *whooduzee whooduzee* think he is?

It's mating season, of course.

He'll be quiet, deathly so,
once summer settles in and the point,
the whole poi-poi-point eludes him.
But for now, like some manic Eliot
on uppers he keeps on, he do
the Police sometimes all night, occasionally
with a bit of nesting material wedged
jauntily in the crook of his beak
like a young tough waggling his Marlboro,
look Ma no mouth,
he warbles, tweets, buzzes, trickles, trills.
He does it so well that every single spring
I'm fooled, I think this one
is different, he'll keep it up all year,
this one does it for sheer love of singing,
loves the zillion singwingednesses of the world
and wants it all to issue from his breast alone,
lightly like a spring bubbling up from the dust,
loves my alarm clock and the rufous-sided towhee
with equal ferocity, this one the true,
true lover, this one the Emil-Emil-Emily
Dickinson of mockingbirds, twirling
ribbons around neat packets of song,
doesn't care if we're listening, me or the ex,
or a current or future mate, or master,
the last mockingbird on the block, doesn't give
a *twat-twit-twat-what?* crow's turd
what comes of his exertions, ruffles then
riffs off again, this time *jay-gull-cardinal-dove
red-winged-blackbird-phoebe-mallard-duck!*

It's month two: by now he's knocked up his share,
come on, by now he's attracted every mockingchick

for acres, miles. What keeps him singing, and what
will stop him? One day in June, one day soon in June.
What caused Emily to tie her final ribbon
in the somehow stiller stillness of her room?

What silences that kind of lover?

What do they know that I don't yet?
How do you *how do you* end
the song that might be your last?

Soldier Lives to Tell

Which one saw which one
first, neither one could know.
What held our weapons
and our gazes fast?
A shock of jet hair
crossed his brow, sweat-
stuck, pointing down
and away. No shame
in hesitation, only danger.
All our training, every nerve
in our fingers, instructed
not to do what we were doing.
Not to not do. But as if he knew
that I could sense the sights
his eyes were filled with,
the nights that cooled him, the days
that built his house, as if he'd sat
in my kitchen, stroked my dog,

  we paused. The seconds curled,
uncurled. We paused.
I could feel my cheek against
his rifle, against the almond-scented
forehead of his son. We didn't

seem to feel the muscle strain
a long-held crouch must cause.
The foliage between us wavered,
subtracted something from the air.
Did we breathe? We watched us there
like two gods who'd forgotten
you can't have two gods
per world, per stretch of field.
Were we scared? We aimed
and stared, struck both by both
our mercy and our might.
And then the lesser of us
started shooting.

Early in Any Century

It is May. The sun fires a continuous volley
of gold through the window. The city
is at peace, the apartment quiet, apart.
Noises in the street are subdued, remote
enough not to notice. You can see
hundreds of windows from this one,
imagine each tenant resting in each lair
since it's a holiday, everyone having
slept in, having by now their second cup
while the wars agitate elsewhere,
chopping up other cities. This
doesn't seem fair until you recall
we have had our own wars, brutal ones,
and we'll have more; it is our turn for gold
sunlight on a yellow chair. Even now
there must be people standing at attention
in museums in this very city, musing
at images of war, amazed by its equipment,
by the stopped clocks and the relics
of burnt flesh so painstakingly preserved,
but let us not neglect this plain yellow chair
whose backrest dazzles like a golden shield
to make a willing Danaë of the eye, the self
retreating a few steps further in denial
of the clamor of the world at arms,

for a while at least, at least for this while,
finding itself above, apart, couchant,
entranced by the dazzling hue.
It is perfectly fair to lounge and stretch
full length in this patch of golden air, war
being elsewhere, and over soon, over there.

Lullaby for End of the Second Millennium

From the point of view of all time,
these recent changes signal
more a return to nature
than a departure, than degradation.
In the beginning, after all,
there was boiling rock.
Then waters arranging their bodies
around an era of softer forms:
lichen, grassland, swaying treetops.
Then creatures, movingly fleshed,
treading pathways that hardened.
Then pavement hardening
and cities, monumental.
Soon mostly rock again,
and radiant. More and more like moon.
Soon, sooner than is being thought,
there will be even more light.
The creatures will have stopped
being able to move
or be moved.
And the rock will boil.

Before You Go

As one before moving to a strange coast
Is moved to plant perennials just
To be, briefly, in spring, remembered,
Still be part of land he can't stand
To think he'll never walk upon again;

As that one's child will press a shell
Into a chink of his closet wall
For the next child moving in to find—
His favorite shell, worn smooth by sand
With spirals that feel funny in your hand;

As a man who loves a woman
Who is leaving him for someone
Will leave a kind note in a book
She might not get around to reading,
Hoping she'll find it listlessly reading

So it strikes her—a spasm of time
Uncoiled—like lightning at the spine
(Though she might find it when she's old,
So much older it seems unreal,
But matters, what he felt and will still feel);

As one who softly sings in the church

Whose walls seem mutely to rehearse
The chants of others, centuries ago;
Who lights her votive taper of song
Feeling calm, unbodied, not alone;

As a mother who commutes will first
Plant silly notes and riddles in verse
Under toys in her son's room
And tucked in the pockets of his pants,
Hoping he won't find them all at once;

I leave these silent words with you,
To whom they may mean next to nothing now.

J. Allyn Rosser has published two previous books of poetry. Her first, *Bright Moves*, won the Morse Poetry Prize; her second, *Misery Prefigured*, won the Crab Orchard Award. She has received the Peter I. B. Lavan Award for Younger Poets from the Academy of American Poets, a Pushcart Prize, and fellowships from the National Endowment for the Arts, the Ohio State Arts Council, and the New Jersey State Council on the Arts. Ms. Rosser holds a Ph.D. in English literature from the University of Pennsylvania and now teaches at Ohio University.

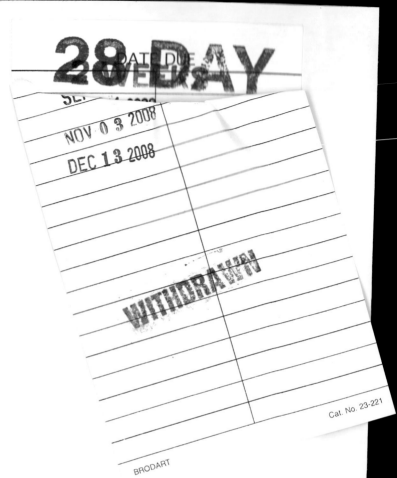